OUCH!

THAT HURTS

Written by Kerrie Shanahan

Flying Start
to Literacy®

CONTENTS

Introduction   4

Broken bones   6

Cuts   11

Stings   14

Burns   18

Summary chart   22

Index   24

INTRODUCTION

Sometimes, your body gets hurt. When this happens, you feel pain and parts of your body might not work well.

The good news is that when your body gets hurt, it can fix itself. You can help your body to get better by looking after it.

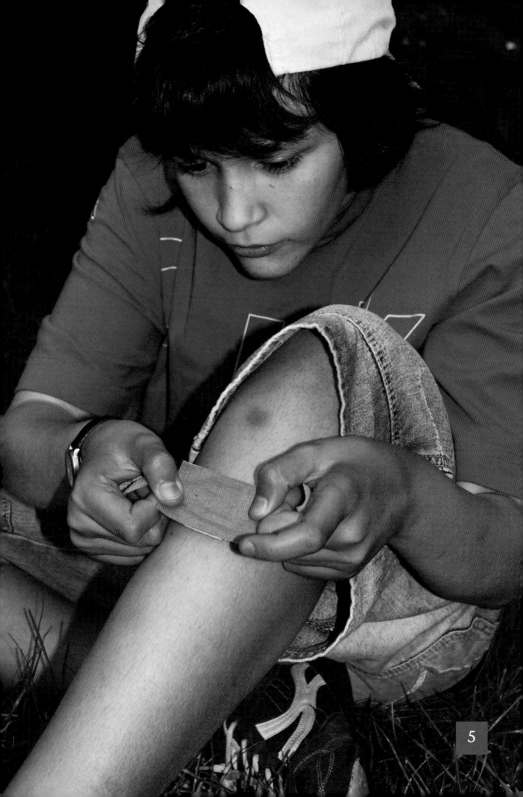

BROKEN BONES

Bones are hard and strong. But sometimes, even bones get broken.

What to do:

- Keep the broken bone still.
- Tell an adult.
- Go to the doctor.

Fracture facts
The place where the bone is broken is called a fracture.

Getting help

A doctor will get an X-ray to see where the bone is broken. A cast is put on the broken leg or arm to hold the bones in place.

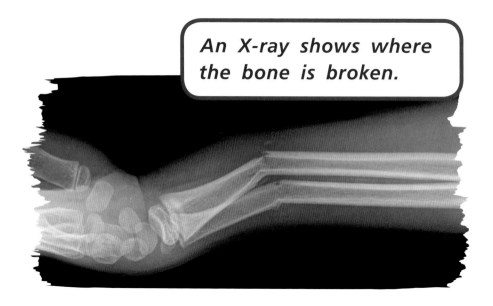

An X-ray shows where the bone is broken.

What happens next?

The broken bones will slowly join together. Most broken bones take six to eight weeks to get better.

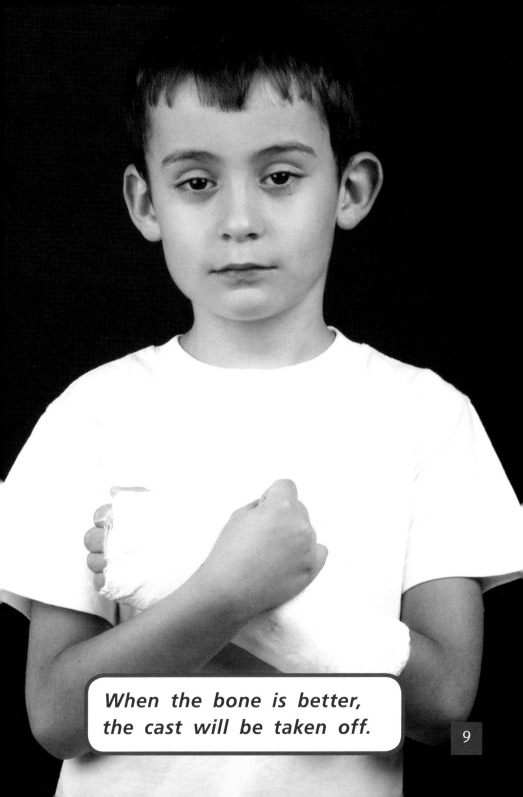

When the bone is better,
the cast will be taken off.

Blood basics

When a cut is bleeding, the blood slowly becomes thicker and sticks together. This is called clotting.

CUTS

Your body is covered in skin and sometimes, skin gets cut.

What to do:
- Press on the cut.
- Tell an adult.
- Clean with water.
- Cover with a bandage.

Getting help

If the cut is deep, go to the doctor. The doctor will clean the cut so that germs cannot get inside. The doctor might use special thread or glue to hold the sides of the cut together, and will then cover it with a bandage.

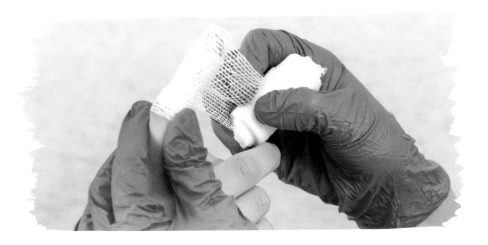

What happens next?

The two sides of the cut that meet will slowly join together. The cut will close up.

STINGS

Sometimes, insects sting people. The sting might hurt or it might be itchy.

You might see a red lump where the insect's sting has gone into your skin.

What to do:

- Tell an adult.
- Put ice on the sting.

Sting alert!

Some people become sick or dizzy and find it hard to breathe when an insect bites them. This is called an allergic reaction.

Getting help

If the sting does not get better, you should go to the doctor. The doctor might give you medicine.

What happens next?

The sting will become less painful and the redness will go away.
Most stings only hurt for a short time.

BURNS

Your skin will burn if you touch something that is very hot.

A burn can be very painful. Your skin will be red and might blister.

What to do:

- Tell an adult.
- Run cool water over the burn.

Sunburn

Sometimes, your skin burns if you get too much sun. You can stop your skin from getting sunburned by wearing a hat and clothes that cover your skin. And don't forget to put on sunscreen.

Getting help

If the burn is large or very bad, you must go to the doctor. The doctor will work out what to do to look after the burn and help your skin get better.

What happens next?

Over time, the redness will disappear. Some burns will get better in about three to six days.

If the burn is very bad, it will take a lot longer to get better. Some deep burns leave a scar on the skin.

SUMMARY CHART

Injury	What to do
Broken bones	• Keep the broken bone still. • Tell an adult. • Go to the doctor.
Cuts	• Press on the cut. • Tell an adult. • Clean with water. • Cover with a bandage.
Stings	• Tell an adult. • Put ice on the sting.
Burns	• Tell an adult. • Run cool water over the burn.

Symptoms	Healing time
• Pain • Swelling • Can't use the limb	• 6 to 8 weeks
• Pain • Blood	• Small cuts heal quickly. • Deep cuts take longer to heal.
• Pain • Itchy • Red lump or swelling	• Most stings get better in a short time.
• Red skin • Blister	• Most burns get better in 3 to 6 days. • Bad burns take longer.

INDEX

allergic reaction 15

blister 18, 22

blood 10, 23

bones 6, 8, 9, 22

cast 8, 9

fracture 7

germs 12

pain 4, 16, 18, 23

scar 21

skin 11, 14, 18,
          20, 21, 23

sunburn 18

X-ray 8